BOLIVIA

in pictures

VISUAL GEOGRAPHY SERIES

By BERNADINE BAILEY

STERLING PUBLISHING CO., INC. NEW YORK

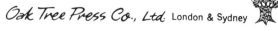

Oak Tree Press Co., Ltd. London & Sydney

VISUAL GEOGRAPHY SERIES

Alaska
Australia
Austria
Belgium and Luxembourg
Berlin—East and West
Bolivia
Brazil
California
Canada
The Caribbean (English-
  Speaking Islands)
Chile
China
Costa Rica
Cuba
Czechoslovakia
Denmark
Dominican Republic
East Germany
Ecuador
Egypt
El Salvador
England
Ethiopia

Fiji
Finland
Florida
France
Ghana
Greece
Guyana
Haiti
Hawaii
Holland
Honduras
Hong Kong
Hungary
Iceland
India
Indonesia
Iran
Iraq
Ireland
Islands of the
  Mediterranean
Israel
Italy
Ivory Coast

Jamaica
Japan
Jordan
Kenya
Korea
Kuwait
Lebanon
Madagascar (Malagasy)
Malawi
Malaysia and Singapore
Mexico
Nepal
New Zealand
Nigeria
Norway
Pakistan and Bangladesh
Panama and the Canal
  Zone
Paraguay
Peru
The Philippines
Poland
Portugal

Puerto Rico
Rhodesia
Russia
Saudi Arabia
Scotland
Senegal
South Africa
Spain
The Sudan
Sweden
Switzerland
Tahiti and the
  French Islands of
  the Pacific
Taiwan
Thailand
Tunisia
Turkey
Uruguay
The U.S.A.
Venezuela
Wales
West Germany

PICTURE CREDITS

The publishers wish to thank the following for the photographs used in this book: Bernadine Bailey; Catholic Foreign Mission Society of America; COMIBOL, Bogotá; Corporacion Boliviana de Vivienda, Bogotá; Franciscan Fathers, Philadelphia; Gulf Oil Corporation; Nathan A. Haverstock, The Latin American Service; ILO; Organization of American States; John Padula; Peace Corps, Washington, D.C.; Lyle Stuart; United Nations; Venezuelan Ministry of Education, Caracas; Hamilton Wright.

A herd of llamas passes along a road near enormous piles of waste from a nearby tin mine.

CONTENTS

1. THE LAND 5
MOUNTAINS . . . THE ALTIPLANO . . . THE YUNGAS . . . THE LOWLANDS (LLANOS) . . . The
Chaco . . . CLIMATE . . . LAKE TITICACA . . . LAKE POOPÓ . . . Salar de Uyuni . . . FLORA AND
FAUNA . . . CITIES . . . La Paz . . . Sucre . . . Cochabamba . . . Santa Cruz . . . Oruro . . . Potosí
. . . Cobija . . . Tarija . . . Trinidad . . . Tiahuanaco
2. HISTORY 23
THE INCA EMPIRE . . . THE COLONIAL ERA . . . THE WAR OF INDEPENDENCE . . . THE
REPUBLIC . . . THE CHACO WAR . . . THE REVOLUTION OF 1952
3. THE GOVERNMENT 30
SUFFRAGE . . . WELFARE SERVICES . . . IMPORTANCE OF LA PAZ . . . POLITICAL PARTIES
4. THE PEOPLE 34
THE WHITE POPULATION . . . THE INDIANS . . . CLOTHING . . . DAILY LIFE . . . FOOD . . .
TRAVELLING DOCTORS . . . FIESTAS . . . LITERATURE . . . EDUCATION
5. THE ECONOMY 48
MINERALS . . . OIL AND GAS . . . AGRICULTURE . . . LIVESTOCK . . . FORESTRY . . . FISHING . . .
MANUFACTURES . . . TRANSPORTATION . . . MANPOWER . . . Trade Unions . . . AID FROM THE
UNITED STATES . . . TOURISM
6. INDEX 64

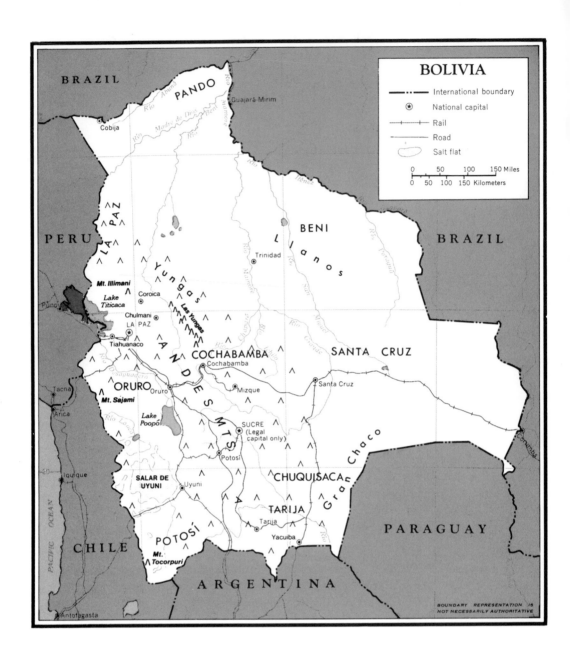

BOLIVIA

International boundary
National capital
Rail
Road
Salt flat

0   50   100   150 Miles
0   50   100   150 Kilometers

BRAZIL

PANDO
Guajará-Mirim
Cobija
Rio Abuná
Rio Madre de Dios

PERU

LA PAZ

Mt. Illimani
Lake Titicaca
Coroica
Chulmani
Yungas
Las Yungas
LA PAZ
Tiahuanaco
Puno

BENI
Llanos
Trinidad

BRAZIL

COCHABAMBA
Cochabamba
Mizque

SANTA CRUZ
Santa Cruz

ORURO
Oruro
Mt. Sajami
Lake Poopó
Tacna
Arica

ANDES MTS.

SUCRE
(Legal capital only)
Potosí

SALAR DE UYUNI
Uyuni

CHUQUISACA

Gran Chaco

PARAGUAY

PACIFIC OCEAN
Iquique

CHILE

POTOSÍ
Mt. Tocorpuri

TARIJA
Tarija
Yacuiba

ARGENTINA

Antofagasta

Corumbá

BOUNDARY REPRESENTATION IS
NOT NECESSARILY AUTHORITATIVE

Mt. Illimani, rising 21,184 feet (6,355 metres) above sea level, provides a snow-covered landmark throughout the year, visible from all parts of La Paz, Bolivia's capital.

I. THE LAND

DEEP IN THE heart of South America lies the landlocked Republic of Bolivia. With an area of 424,163 square miles (1,098,000 sq. km.), Bolivia is almost twice the size of Texas and three and one half times as large as the British Isles.

This large country has no seacoast of its own —it is hemmed in by other countries on all sides. North and east of Bolivia is the vast expanse of Brazil, while Paraguay borders Bolivia on the south and east. Directly south is Argentina, and on the west are Peru and Chile.

Since it is both mountainous and landlocked, Bolivia is sometimes called the "Switzerland of South America." Paraguay, the only other South American country that does not touch the sea, is not mountainous.

MOUNTAINS

Three great ranges of the Andes Mountains cut across Bolivia, extending 500 miles (804 kilometres) from the northwest to the southeast, and towering to heights of over 20,000 feet (6,000 metres). The one farthest west is the

A Peace Corps volunteer teaches modern methods of sheep shearing to Indians in the village of Chirapaca, about an hour's drive from La Paz on the windswept Altiplano. The shepherd's little woollen cap is worn widely by the Indians of Bolivia and other Andean countries.

These Indian women work at the Milluni Mine, at an altitude of 15,000 feet (4,600 metres)!

These Indian homes in the highlands near La Paz are fortunate in having many trees nearby to keep out the cold winds.

Cordillera Occidental ("occidental" means western in Spanish), the middle range is the Cordillera Real ("real" means royal), and the eastern one is the Cordillera Oriental (eastern).

Some cows mother their new calves on a large estate near Santa Cruz. Cattle are raised chiefly in the Yungas and in the lowlands, as they are not adapted to the high altitudes.

THE ALTIPLANO

Between and flanking the mountain ranges are plateaus 12,000 feet (3,600 metres) high—the Altiplano. There is only one other place in the world where people live on land as high as this—Tibet, in central Asia. It is not easy to live at such an altitude, because of the cold and the lack of oxygen in the air.

Snow-topped mountains shoot thousands of feet toward the sky from their bases on these high plateaus. Four mountain peaks in Bolivia rank among the highest in the world. On the Chilean border is Mt. Tocorpuri, 22,162 feet (6,486 metres), the highest in Bolivia. The next three highest are Sajama (21,555 feet or 6,466 metres), Ancohuma (21,490 feet or 6,447 metres), and Illimani (21,184 feet or 6,355 metres).

THE YUNGAS

Between the high Andes in the west and the lowlands of the east, there is a third region. This middle section, called the *Yungas*, is made up of lower mountains and very deep valleys. This region is "middle" in every way—in its location, in the height of its mountains, and in its temperate climate.

Most of Bolivia's crops are grown in the

7

The swamps and jungles of the lowlands, with their dense vegetation, make progress difficult in eastern Bolivia.

Yungas. The plateau region, or Altiplano, is too high and cold. The lowlands, or Llanos, are, for the most part, too hot and rainy for anything except tropical plants.

THE LOWLANDS (LLANOS)

In northern and eastern Bolivia there are no mountain ranges and high plateaus—instead, the land is low and flat. Several rivers rise in the high Andes, fed by the mountain snows, and flow northward through the low country and eventually join the Madeira River of Brazil, which empties into the mighty Amazon. Smaller rivers that also start in the Andes of Bolivia flow southward to join the giant Plata River of Argentina. None of the Bolivian rivers empties into the Pacific Ocean. The few that flow westward either disappear into the soil or feed the two large lakes of Bolivia.

THE CHACO

The southern edge of the Llanos merges into the Bolivian part of a vast arid region, the Gran Chaco, most of which lies in Paraguay and Argentina.

Every day, during the dry season, this young girl of the Chaco region has to take her donkey to a spring 7 miles (11 km.) away to get water.

These Indian children live in the town of Laja, near La Paz, where it is cool enough to wear wool caps and heavy pullovers.

CLIMATE

Because of its location in the torrid zone, between the Equator and the Tropic of Capricorn, one would expect this country to have a warm, tropical climate throughout. The high altitude, however, of much of the land makes the climate there much cooler than is usual in the tropics. The temperature in the highlands never goes above 75° or 77° F. (25° C.).

Bolivia has every gradation of temperature, from that of the tropical lowlands to the Arctic cold of the snow-capped peaks. Instead of having four seasons, as in the temperate zone, Bolivia has two—a rainy season and a dry season. During the three months of the rainy season—December, January, and February—it is usually rainy and cold in the morning, maybe as low as 40° F. (4.4° C.). By noon, however, the skies may clear and the sun will shine the rest of the day. In the northeast part of the country, rain falls throughout the year, but the summer months (November-March) are usually described as the rainy season.

LAKE TITICACA

Lying partly in Bolivia and partly in Peru, Lake Titicaca is the second largest lake in South America, covering an area of 3,200 square miles (8,320 sq. km.). At 12,506 feet (3,751 metres) above sea level, it is the highest lake in the world on which steamboats operate. The lake is 138 miles (221 km.) long and 69

Indian homes on the shores of Lake Titicaca have thatched roofs and walls of stone and adobe.

Lake Titicaca, which Bolivia shares with Peru, is one of the country's most valuable assets, providing fish for local consumption and also many attractions for visitors.

miles (110 km.) wide, and the shore line is indented with many bays and coves. Its waters are unusually clear and reflect the blue of the sky. The lake has 36 islands, of which the largest is the Island of the Sun and the Moon.

The Indians living near the lake make their own boats, which look something like canoes, from a reed, *totora*, that grows on the lake shore. Such a boat, called a *balsa*, lasts only five months, but it is used every day, especially for fishing. As a rule, only two people ride in a *balsa*, though it can actually hold four. For a short trip, small sails of reed are attached to the *balsa*, while for a long trip, cloth sails are used.

LAKE POOPÓ

This lake, fed principally by the outflow of water from Lake Titicaca, lies 180 miles (288 km.) southeast of the larger lake, and is 505 feet (151 metres) lower. With an area of 386 square miles (1,103 sq. km.), Lake Poopó has one large inhabited island. The lake itself is shallow and its shores are sparsely populated.

SALAR DE UYUNI

South of Lake Poopó is the Salar de Uyuni, a vast salt-marsh several times larger than the lake itself.

FLORA AND FAUNA

The llama, alpaca, vicuña, and guanaco, all relatives of the camel, rank among the most interesting of all animals native to Bolivia. The first two were domesticated by the Indians long before the discovery of America. These animals are highly prized for their silky fleece, which is used in making the finest overcoats. The wild guanaco is hunted for its skin which,

These canoe-like boats, called "balsas," are made of a local reed and are widely used by the Indians on Lake Titicaca.

The llama is the typical animal of the highlands, where it serves as a beast of burden as well as a source of wool, meat, and leather. Its importance is diminishing, however, due to the introduction of modern vehicles.

The alpaca, a close relative of the llama, is too small for a pack animal, but is raised for its fine wool, which is sent to many parts of the world for manufacture into cloth.

The condor, a large vulture with a wingspread of 10 feet (3.4 metres), lives in the high Andes. These two specimens live in the outdoor museum of La Paz, where many kinds of native animals may be found.

when dressed, makes an attractive rug or robe, and the vicuña, also wild, is highly prized for its lustrous wool.

Besides many species of monkeys that live in the tropical forests, the lowlands also are home to the puma, jaguar, wildcat, coati, tapir, sloth, and ant-bear. The spectacled bear, a rare species, is found among the wooded foothills of the Andes. There are several species of deer, but they are not numerous. The armadillo, opossum, otter, and skunk are widely distributed. In the warm, tropical lowlands many alligators, lizards, and turtles lurk, along with numerous snakes, including rattlers (pit-vipers) and the giant boa constrictor.

In the high altitudes are many condors and eagles of the largest size, while the common vulture is found throughout the country. The rhea or American ostrich and a species of large stork live in the tropical plains and valleys. Many species of humming-birds are found high in the mountains, while great numbers of parrots and toucans brighten the forests of the lowlands.

Because of the great variety in climate,

Bolivia's vegetation ranges from scanty Arctic-type trees and flowers to the lush forests of the tropics. In between these extremes, a great variety of fruits and vegetables grow, including those found in the temperate zone as well as in the tropics.

The warm lowland region produces many valuable trees, especially the rubber tree and the cinchona tree. An important drug—quinine—is made from the bark of the cinchona. Only one other country in South America—Brazil—exports more rubber than Bolivia does.

The vicuña, a wild relative of the llama, is becoming very rare, and hence more valuable, because it cannot be bred in captivity. Its fur is made into the finest grade of cloth, used widely in making overcoats.

La Paz, highest capital city in the world, lies in a bowl surrounded by barren mountains, with snow-capped peaks in the distance. It is a dramatic situation, but with hazards for those who are not used to the rarefied air. Because of the surrounding mountains, La Paz has little room to spread out. It has already started climbing up the foothills.

CITIES

LA PAZ

The seat of the national government, La Paz, is one of the most unusual cities in the world—it is 12,000 feet high (3,600 metres), and yet it is in the bottom of a canyon! Steep mountains form a snow-capped wall around the city, which lies in a valley 3 miles (4.8 km.) wide and 10 miles (16 km.) long. No other capital city in the world is as high as this one. People who are not used to such altitudes become out of breath very soon when walking on the steep streets of La Paz. One has to walk very slowly and stop often to rest.

In the thin, clear air of the plateau, the city of La Paz shines like a bright jewel. Yellow stucco houses, red tile roofs, patches of green trees, sparkling streams, and the brilliant flower market—all combine to make a scene of vivid beauty. The climate is dry and very pleasant half of the year, but humid and cold from November to March—the rainy season.

With a population of more than 500,000, La Paz is by far the largest city in Bolivia. Many of the people are Spanish-speaking-whites, many more are Indians, and some are a mixture of the two, called *Cholos*.

South Americans like to name their streets for important dates in the history of their country. In La Paz, for example, there is the 20th of October Avenue, named for the day in 1548 of the city's founding by the Spanish captain, Alonso de Mendoza. There is also the

13

The beautiful 16th of July Avenue, with its esplanade, is the most important street in La Paz.

16th of July Avenue, named for the day in 1809 when the movement for independence was started. It is easy to learn historical dates in a city such as this.

The market place of La Paz is the liveliest part of the city. A daily market is held indoors, with large stalls for selling vegetables, fruits, meats, flowers, and other items. The Indian

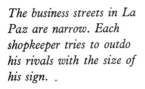

The business streets in La Paz are narrow. Each shopkeeper tries to outdo his rivals with the size of his sign.

Street markets, which are quite numerous in La Paz, carry all kinds of household necessities, such as dishes, pans, and brooms. The Indian women come to the market very early in the morning, usually walking several miles from their farm homes. No wonder they like to sit while tending shop.

women in charge of the stalls sit on a sort of shelf, often with their children, and spend their spare time knitting or sewing. The market is full of strange contrasts—llamas that have come from the north, bearing loads of ice, and mules from the south, laden with oranges and other tropical fruits.

The cathedral faces the Plaza Murillo, the main square of the city, as is customary in Spanish towns. This is the largest cathedral in all South America, built mainly of marble and with a magnificent altar. Next door is the

Even in the indoor market, surrounded by fresh vegetables, the Indian women wear their characteristic bowler, or derby, hats.

15

In La Paz, the open-air theatre of the University is used for plays and concerts throughout much of the year.

Presidential Palace, and on the opposite side of the plaza is the Capitol, where the two chambers of the National Congress meet. The Iglesia San Francisco, finished in the 17th century, is the oldest church in La Paz, and one of the oldest in all South America.

In the beautiful residential section of Miraflores, there are fine houses, where the well-to-do professional and business people live. The Indians live mostly in adobe houses on the hillside.

The University of San Andres occupies a

Modern houses and apartments are to be found in the more prosperous sections of La Paz.

The Church of Maria Auxiliadora, in La Paz, shows the trend toward a more modern style of architecture, as distinct from the classical. The dark cone at the lower left is a carefully pruned tree.

Many Indians live in narrow cobblestone streets in La Paz. The buildings that line this street, however, were originally built as fine homes for wealthy Spaniards.

large building in the heart of La Paz. In front of the University there is a large outdoor arena, where concerts or plays are given every Sunday, except during the winter months. There is also an outdoor museum, with exhibits of pre-Inca culture, and a park filled with native mammals and birds.

La Paz was the first city in South America to have electric street lights. Smooth, well paved avenues are found in the newer sections of the city, while narrow, steep little streets paved with old cobblestones are found in other parts. The better residential area is somewhat limited.

Due to the high altitude, little oxygen is present in the air, and hence a fire is a great rarity—therefore the city does not have a fire department.

In the outdoor museum of La Paz stands this ancient monolith, with hieroglyphs that have never been deciphered.

At a railway station near Cochabamba, open-air lunch counters do a brisk business.

SUCRE

Lying high in the mountains of south-central Bolivia is the old city of Sucre, founded in 1538. Originally called Chuquisaca, the name was changed in 1825 to Sucre, after General Sucre, who won the battle that gained independence for Bolivia.

Sucre was the first capital of Bolivia, but today the real seat of government is La Paz. The Supreme Court is the only department of government that now meets in Sucre, although the Congress Building, where Independence was declared on August 6, 1825, has been preserved in its original condition.

The city is relatively small, with only 60,000 people, and has a delightful climate throughout the year. Sucre has its own airport as well as a railway that links it with Potosí and a good highway to Cochabamba and to Santa Cruz. The famous University of San Javier, where many leaders of the 19th century were educated, has continued to maintain its traditional prestige. Commercial enterprises include a cement factory and an oil refinery.

COCHABAMBA

Dating from 1571, Cochabamba today has 149,000 people and is the second most important city in the republic. It lies midway between La Paz and Santa Cruz, occupying a fertile plateau between the central and eastern ranges of mountains. Its climate is considered one of the best in the world, with very little change throughout the year. Winter does not really exist here, and in summer the temperature is never unpleasantly high—the people can wear the same type of clothes throughout the year.

Cochabamba is typically Spanish, with its large central plaza, surrounded on four sides by buildings with arcades. The University of San Simón is the hub of cultural activity, and there are also several military schools.

The city is in the middle of a rich farming area, which has earned it the name of "the granary of Bolivia." It is important for trading in grains and other products grown on the plateau. Industry is growing rapidly and several new factories have been opened. With

A nondescript modern structure adjoins buildings of the colonial period in the main plaza in Santa Cruz.

its central location, its fine climate, and other conditions suitable for growth, Cochabamba is considered the city of the future in Bolivia.

SANTA CRUZ

Founded in 1560, Santa Cruz de la Sierra today has a population of 150,000, having grown faster than any other Bolivian city in recent years. A railway line joins Santa Cruz with Corumbo, to the east. Yacuiba to the south, and Cochabamba on the west. A fine highway also links Santa Cruz and Cochabamba.

Situated in the middle of the tropical zone, the city has an extremely hot climate during most of the year. In the winter, however, cold winds called *Surazos* come from the mountains.

Most of the people living in Santa Cruz are of pure Spanish descent, since the original Indian tribes who lived there were killed off a long time ago.

ORURO

Just north of Lake Poopó, in western Bolivia, is the city of Oruro, which owes its existence to

The Cathedral in Santa Cruz adjoins government buildings to the right, where the official business of the Department (province) is carried on.

This street in Potosí is lined with typically Spanish buildings, whose balconies overhang the street.

the discovery of silver mines. Founded in 1606, it now has a population of 90,000.

Silver was mined there in colonial days, but now tin and copper are the principal products. Nearby are a number of thermal springs, whose waters are said to be helpful in curing various diseases.

The Technical University of St. Augustine has a faculty of mining engineering, the oldest in Bolivia, and, under the auspices of the United Nations, there is an Institute of Metallurgical Investigation. About two miles from Oruro, a tin foundry was opened in 1970.

POTOSÍ

A few miles southwest of Sucre, on a plateau even higher than La Paz, is the old city of Potosí. The King of Spain gave it the title of "Royal Imperial City of Potosí." It was here, in 1545, that an Indian, Diego Huallpa, discovered the richest silver mine in the world.

Its fame soon spread, and people flocked here from all regions to exploit its riches. They began to build homes without any plan or order. During the colonial period, when great fortunes in silver were being taken from the

In Potosí, the Cathedral faces the main plaza of the town, as is customary in old Spanish cities.

20

mines, Potosí had a population of 160,000—now it has about 70,600. After 400 years of mining, the silver is long since gone, but Potosí is now prospering from mining tin and other metals.

COBIJA

In the extreme north, on the border of Brazil, is the city of Cobija, one of the newer settlements. Founded in 1906, it has 15,000 people. Cobija is located in an area producing rubber, cacao, almonds, and other tropical products. It is also in a fine locality for hunting and fishing.

TARIJA

In the extreme south is the town of Tarija, with 35,000 people. During the colonial period, it was the site of many religious missions, especially of the Jesuits and Franciscans. Today, Tarija is important for its oil wells and the refining of sugar.

A stone from the Tiahuanaco ruins is proudly displayed by a native of the region.

TRINIDAD

Located slightly north of the exact midpoint of Bolivia, the old city of Trinidad, founded in 1686 by the Jesuits, has 20,000 inhabitants. During the rainy season, Trinidad becomes an island when the rivers overflow their banks. It is the hub of the cattle-raising area of Bolivia.

TIAHUANACO

On the shores of Lake Titicaca lies Tiahuanaco, Bolivia's city of mystery. No one knows the story of this old, old city—it goes back to the days before history was written. It was once beautiful, with large, impressive

Workers are carrying on excavations in the ruins of Tiahuanaco, but vast areas of the mysterious city still remain to be unearthed.

buildings, but now it is only a mass of ghostly ruins. Tiahuanaco was built by a race that has completely vanished, a race that lived long before the days of the Incas. From its fine old ruins one can gain some idea of the beauty that was once a part of the ancient civilization of South America. Perhaps the most impressive of Tiahuanaco's ruins is the huge stone gateway, known as the Gate of the Sun. At the top of the gateway is a large carving of the Sun God, bearing a double sceptre and ruling an army of 48 lesser figures. Through the centuries this stone ruin has become cracked, but it remains an impressive memorial of a civilization that existed thousands of years ago.

The central figure of the Gateway of the Sun is believed to represent the Sun God.

The Gateway of the Sun is the most impressive feature of the ruins of Tiahuanaco.

2. HISTORY

FROM HUMAN REMAINS and the bones of animals, scientists believe that mankind lived in the area that is now Bolivia at least 10,000 years ago. The first known inhabitants, however, were the Tiahuanacotas, who lived on the south shore of Lake Titicaca at least 500 years before the Christian era. These people left undeciphered hieroglyphs. The remains of their civilization have not been excavated or studied fully, so the history and traditions of their way of life are not known to us. The existing remains of huge stone structures, however, show great technical perfection. Stones weighing more than 100 tons had been accurately cut and ground to a smooth finish. These ancient people had undoubtedly attained a high degree of civilization, with a centralized control, both political and religious.

One marvels at the skill of the people of ancient Tiahuanaco, who moved stones much larger than this 35-ton (32-metric-ton) slab, after cutting them with precision and carving designs and messages on them. These men are soldiers working under the supervision of archeologists.

THE INCA EMPIRE

This empire was founded, according to tradition, in the year 1160 by one Manco Capac and his wife, Mama Ocllo. Throughout their history, the Incas were ruled by a single dynastic family, but in a welfare-state sort of way. Each year the officials estimated the amount of land that could be cultivated and allotted to each family the land needed to provide it with sufficient food. The rest of the land was allotted to the state or the state religion, and the peasants were required to cultivate it before their own.

Despite a lack of modern tools, the Incas constructed aqueducts and irrigation systems, carried out involved surveying work, and built roads and suspension bridges.

During the 15th century, the Incas began a campaign of expansion that within a hundred years made them masters of an empire that stretched 2,000 miles along the west coast of South America and probably included 4,500,000 people. By the year 1500, they had conquered

an uncounted number of tribes, with different languages and customs, and united them into one of the great empires of all time. The highlands of present-day Bolivia comprised the Inca province of Kollasuyu. In the lowlands to the east of the Andes there were scattered tribes that were never conquered by the Incas. The last Inca leader, Atahuallpa, was taken prisoner by the Spaniards in 1532, and in spite of the fabulous amount of gold and silver given in ransom to the conquistador Pizarro, he was never released.

THE COLONIAL ERA

When Columbus discovered America in 1492, the Inca Empire had reached its greatest extent. But when a small Spanish ship, with 130 foot soldiers and 40 horsemen, sailed from Panama in 1527 in search of the famed riches of the Andes, the downfall of the Inca Empire had begun. In 1532, the Spaniards, led by Francisco Pizarro and Diego de Almagro, conquered the Incas, and in 1534 the two conquerors divided the empire between themselves. Pizarro took the northern part of the territory, and Almagro the southern. One small group of Incas, on the eastern slopes of the Andes, resisted the conquerors for another 40 years.

The Spanish conquerors brought their language and customs, their religion and culture, which are reflected in the literature and architecture of Bolivia today.

Early in the period of Spanish rule, the mines of Potosí were discovered, the richest silver mines in the world, and their discovery had far-reaching consequences for Bolivia. Eager for gold and silver, the Spaniards forced large numbers of Indians to leave the land and work in the mines. The rich mines around Potosí

In the early days of Spanish colonial rule, the wealthy families all had a hacienda, or large farmhouse, usually enclosed by a wall. Near the main house itself there were trees and graceful archways.

soon became the principal source of wealth for Spain. The city's population grew to 160,000 by 1650.

Throughout the 16th century, the Spaniards continued their exploration and settlement of the land they had conquered. In those days, the region that is now Bolivia was known as Upper Peru. During this period most of the Bolivian cities were founded. In 1538, the seat of government was established at Charcas, later called La Plata, then called Chuquisaca, and finally named Sucre, after General Sucre, the second president of the republic. A high court of justice was set up here in 1559. The silver mountain of Potosí, then synonymous with fabulous riches, is represented on the coat-of-arms of Bolivia today.

When private ownership of land was permitted, large haciendas (estates) became the dominant institution, and a land-owning aristocracy developed. The Indians were allowed to farm small plots of land, paying for this privilege by working several days a week in the fields of the landlord. They also had to contribute firewood, eggs, and many other goods and services.

In the late 1700's, there was a series of insurrections among the Indians of the Andes, who tried to drive out the Europeans and re-establish the Inca Empire. Some 40,000 Indians besieged La Paz for more than 100 days, in 1781, but were finally suppressed. Never again did the Indians try to regain their former territory.

months later, Bolívar's lieutenant, General Antonio José de Sucre, won the battle of Ayacucho in Peru. This marked the end of Spanish rule in Bolivia and Peru.

THE REPUBLIC

On August 6, 1825, what had formerly been Alto (Upper) Peru now became an independent republic. It was named Bolivia in honor of the great liberator. General Bolívar himself drafted a constitution that was ratified by a new Congress in 1826.

Simón Bolívar was elected the first president, but he remained in office for only six months. During this period he showed his genius as an administrator. General Sucre succeeded Bolívar as president and held office for two and a half years. The memory of both men is greatly cherished by all Bolivians.

The first native-born president of Bolivia was Andres Santa Cruz, the son of a Spanish official and Maria Calahumana, a direct descendant of the last Inca. He formed a confederation of Peru and Bolivia, but this combination aroused the jealousy of Chile, Argentina, and Brazil. Santa Cruz was defeated by Chile in the battle of Yungay, the confederation was destroyed in 1839, and Santa Cruz was exiled.

For the next 40 years, Bolivia was a land of constant strife and insurrection, where dictators wrecked the economy and robbed the people. The country was finally forced to surrender all of its territory bordering on the Pacific to Chile. In return, Chile built a railway from the port of Arica to La Paz and agreed to carry Bolivian goods free to certain ports. Bolivia has never resigned itself to the loss of its ports, and has ever since sought to get them back from Chile.

THE WAR OF INDEPENDENCE

The idea of independence from Spain had been growing for some years. The first action for Spanish-American independence came on May 25, 1809, when the people of Chuquisaca revolted and established their own government. This set in motion similar uprisings in La Paz, Cochabamba, Oruro, Potosí, and Santa Cruz.

For almost 15 years there was open warfare between the Spaniards who had come from Europe and the Creoles, those of Spanish descent born in America. The Creoles tried desperately to overthrow the Spanish authority, but the royalist forces always turned them back. At the same time, local leaders who were really bandits fought for wealth and power. During the course of these combats and skirmishes, the Spanish power was gradually weakened.

The fate of Bolivia and Peru was decided by General Simón Bolívar. After his victories in Venezuela, Colombia, and Ecuador, Bolívar entered Peru and won another victory on the plains of Junin on August 6, 1824. Four

General Antonio José de Sucre, one of the liberators of South America and the second president of Bolivia, gave his name to the nation's legal capital.

When a tremendous demand for rubber came in 1900, it brought immense wealth to the jungle state of Acre, which then declared itself independent. Bolivia was unable to subdue the secessionists, who were armed by Brazil. As a result, most of the area was given to Brazil in 1903, in return for a cash settlement.

During World War I, Bolivia's tin mining and cattle raising brought a tremendous economic boom to the country. Bolivia sold only to the Allies, and broke off relations with Germany in 1917, when a ship carrying a Bolivian minister was torpedoed. Bolivia was represented at the Versailles Peace Conference and became a charter member of the League of Nations.

This statue of Simón Bolívar, the liberator, stands in a prominent place on the 16th of July Avenue in La Paz.

THE CHACO WAR

After World War I, the economic boom continued, based largely on oil. There was no political stability, however, as one leader after another formed a new party, led a revolt and a coup, only to be in turn overthrown by someone else a year or two later. In addition, there were border clashes with Paraguay over the oil-rich Gran Chaco area, in the southeast. These clashes led to full-scale warfare in 1932 and a treaty in 1938. Bolivia lost another 90,000 square miles (225,000 sq. km.) of territory, and both nations suffered heavy losses of wealth and manpower.

The Chaco War, however, brought about important changes in the military, political, and cultural life of Bolivia. All young men now faced military conscription, which brought together whites, Indians and *Cholos* (mixed) in a way that had not happened before. For the first time, the Indians became aware of their own political rôle. After attempts on the part of

27

Map legend:
- Original extent of Bolivia
- To Brazil 1867
- To Brazil 1903
- To Peru 1909
- To Brazil 1902
- To Brazil 1867
- BRAZIL
- BOLIVIA
- To Paraguay 1938
- To Chile 1884, 1894
- PERU
- Pacific Ocean
- CHILE
- ARGENTINA
- PARAGUAY

Bolivia at the time of its becoming independent laid claim to a much larger territory than it has today. A succession of wars with the surrounding countries led to the loss of Bolivia's seacoast and vast tracts of the Chaco and the Amazonian lowlands. The most serious loss was that of Atacama with its seaport of Antofagasta and its rich nitrate deposits.

several reforming presidents to turn the republic into a socialist state, the older military generation returned to power in 1940, under General Enrique Penaranda.

THE REVOLUTION OF 1952

The many political coups in Bolivian history had not changed the basic set-up, whereby the wealthy white landowners and the military men ran the country. More than half the population did not even speak Spanish, but worked hard on the farms and in the mines, producing the food and exports for the entire country. Among the political organizations that sprang up after the Chaco War, the National Revolutionary Movement (MNR) eventually became the most powerful, after a brief and bloody revolt in April, 1952. The Revolutionary Movement made sweeping changes—the army was reduced in size, universal voting began, the Indians were granted civil rights, and the largest mines were taken over by the government. Through a land reform plan, the peasants were given small tracts of land for their own use, and attempts were made to educate the Indians. The rich

landowners thus lost much of their power and wealth.

With financial aid from the United States, the MNR remained in power until 1964. During this period they carried out undertakings that were of great economic benefit. Railways were built from Brazil and Argentina to Santa Cruz, a substantial road was built from Santa Cruz and Cochabamba to the market cities in the highlands, and tracts of jungle were converted into farmland. Unfortunately, in 1965, the MNR split into quarrelling factions, and a military government took over the republic. By this time, however, the state monopoly of oil, the agricultural expansion, and the more attractive conditions for foreign investment had begun to attract capital and to strengthen the economy.

Early in 1967, guerrilla activity against the government broke out in the southeast. It was thought that the Cuban leader, Fidel Castro, had inspired this activity by sending in Communist agitators, under the leadership of Che Guevara. They never won the support of the peasants, however, and never posed a real threat to the national government.

With the aid of U.S. military advisers, the Bolivian Army and the peasants smashed the guerrilla movement. Che Guevara was wounded and captured on October 8, 1967, and shot to death the next day.

When President Barrientos was killed in a helicopter crash on April 27, 1969, he was succeeded by Vice-President Luis Adolfo Siles Salinas. The country still remained in a somewhat unsettled state, and the new president was ousted on September 26, 1969, and General Alfredo Ovando Candia assumed the

presidency. In 1970, Ovando was overthrown by a leftist coup led by General Juan José Torres. Torres in turn was ousted by General Hugo Bánzer Suárez, head of a right-wing and moderate coalition. The Bánzer régime had to deal with numerous insurrections and wildcat strikes after it assumed power.

Bánzer's rule was most seriously challenged in January, 1974, when a peasant revolt broke out after the general had ordered price increases during a food shortage. The revolt was quickly quelled, but was followed by strikes and mass arrests.

In 1977, Bánzer announced that constitutional government would be restored and that elections would be held in 1978. The elections took place in July, 1978, and General Juan Pereda Asbún appeared to be the winner. However, an electoral court threw out the results on the grounds that the election was rigged. President Bánzer declared a state of siege, then resigned and turned over power to Asbún. Bolivia had a new president, but a return to democratic procedures seemed remote.

The Asbún régime, however, was overthrown in a bloodless coup in November, 1978, carried out by army officers. A three-man junta was put in power, headed by General David Padilla Arancibia, who announced that democratic elections would be held on July 1, 1979. Asbún's support had come mostly from conservatives and the air force. The new régime was composed of army officers regarded as moderate or liberal.

The Palacio Legislativo, or Congress Building, in La Paz houses the Senate and the Chamber of Deputies.

3. THE GOVERNMENT

THE GOVERNMENT of Bolivia has been run by decree since 1969. The following description applies to constitutional government.

Like most republics, Bolivia has executive, legislative, and judicial branches, each theoretically independent. The executive power is in the hands of the president, who is elected for a term of four years. He appoints a cabinet of 15 members. The president and vice-president are elected by direct popular vote, and as a rule they cannot be elected for a second term immediately. When President Victor Paz was elected to succeed himself in 1964, it caused a revolt which resulted in General René Barrientos becoming president in December of that year. The president is required by law to make a tour of the country at least once during his term of office, in order to study the needs of the people.

Legislative authority is in the hands of a Congress, consisting of a Senate and a Chamber of Deputies. Congress meets once a year, for a session of 90 days. The entire country is divided into nine departments, or states, and the Senate has three members from each department, or 27 in all. They are elected by the people and serve for 6 years. One-third of the members are elected every two years.

The Chamber of Deputies has 102 members, elected for 4 years. Half the members of the Chamber are elected every two years.

Each of the nine departments of Bolivia is governed by a *prefect*, appointed by the president for a 4-year term. The departments are sub-divided into provinces, each one under the authority of a *sub-prefect*, who is also appointed by the president. The provinces, in turn, are divided into cantons, each governed by a *corregidor*, who is chosen by the prefect. Each city has a *mayor*, appointed by the president, and a city council elected by the people.

The government of the entire country is thus kept firmly in the hands of the national president, since he appoints the prefects, the sub-prefects, and the mayors.

Although Sucre is the legal capital of Bolivia, the seat of government is actually La Paz, where all legislative and executive functions are carried on. Only the Supreme Court meets in Sucre, as has been pointed out.

SUFFRAGE

Before July 21, 1952, only men who could read and write were allowed to vote in national elections. In 1952, however, the right to vote was given to all citizens, both men and women, who had reached the age of 20. Even those who cannot read are able to vote intelligently, since each party has its own special color for its ballots. This method has proven very successful, and more and more Indians eagerly take part in the general elections.

The Municipal Library in La Paz is a modern building with very tall, fluted columns at the entrance.

A clinic in La Paz treats poor people, as part of the government welfare services.

WELFARE SERVICES

Bolivia has very modern welfare services. Its social security plan provides for health and maternity benefits, for compensation to workmen who are injured during the course of their work, and family allowances for those who are unable to work. It has long been felt that new public services are needed in the fields of health and sanitation. The government has been working in co-operation with the United Nations and the United States to achieve these objectives.

IMPORTANCE OF LA PAZ

During 150 years of independence, the republic of Bolivia has had a turbulent political history. Hardly a 5-year period has passed that has not seen a major political uprising—sometimes there have been two or more in a single year. Most of these occurred in the city of La Paz, and left the rest of the country undisturbed.

Actually, the city of La Paz wields a great deal of political power, more than that of many other capital cities of the world. All political parties are formed in La Paz and have their headquarters here. Any political leader of more than local importance lives in La Paz or keeps

a residence there for a good part of the year. All major candidates for office, including Senators and Deputies, are nominated from La Paz, even if they are running for office in some distant department.

Most of the political uprisings in La Paz have found staunch support among the Indians and the *Cholos*. Feeling very insecure because of their race, they can usually be relied upon to defy the central government in return for any promise to better their own condition. They have never learned that the real trouble lies in the system, and that a change of leadership makes very little difference.

The Army has played a vital rôle in the political upheavals in Bolivia, since all but a few of the country's revolutions have come about through a military takeover.

POLITICAL PARTIES

There are usually as many as 6 to 10 major political parties, and others spring up whenever there is a general election. This means that a candidate for the presidency must gain the support of a number of parties in order to be elected. In order to please a number of different parties, a candidate must make all kinds of contradictory promises. There can scarcely be any single, clear-cut issue. When

The Inter-American Development Bank has contributed funds to modernize the nationalized mines of Bolivia, such as the one seen here.

he takes office, the president is forced to make many compromises. If he cannot please a majority, his position of leadership is threatened, and he may even be forced to resign—or he may be overthrown. This situation tends to keep Bolivia in a constant state of political turmoil.

A typical example of how this system operates is shown in the case of General Torres. In 1970, the left-wing forces of Bolivia found expression. After a week of political upsets, the left-wing General Torres took over the presidency on October 7. The businessmen of Bolivia did not like President Torres' drive against foreign firms, who played a very important part in the country's economy. They did not approve of the government taking over the Bolivian Gulf Oil Company and the sugar industry. Also they were angry because President Torres gave in to the demands of the workers for higher wages and because he expelled the U.S. Peace Corps from Bolivia. Also, President Torres had said that Bolivia would recognize Communist Cuba, in line with a policy of establishing relations with all countries.

After four days of bloody fighting between left-wing students and workers on one side and Army detachments led by right-wing officers on the other, President Torres was replaced on August 22, 1971, by Colonel Hugo Bánzer, formerly head of the Military Academy. The rightist military forces claimed that they were saving the country from Communism. Under President Bánzer, the government began getting aid from Brazil to build new roads and railway lines.

For the most part, the head of state in Bolivia serves not from election to election, but from coup to coup. In this situation, the military plays a more important part than the voters in choosing the president. When a president is overthrown by a coup, he has to take refuge in the embassy of some other country, usually Argentina or Paraguay.

After he was in office, President Bánzer described his régime as a "revolutionary nationalist" government, and he promised to re-establish "respect for the law" and to safeguard foreign investments. The left-wing attitude of the former Torres administration, however, had undermined business confidence. A long-term scheme for industry was announced, and a U.S. $12,000,000 tin smelter was opened at Vinto. The nationalization of the big tin-mining enterprises had taken away their economic and political influence and had given control of the most important resources of the country to the government.

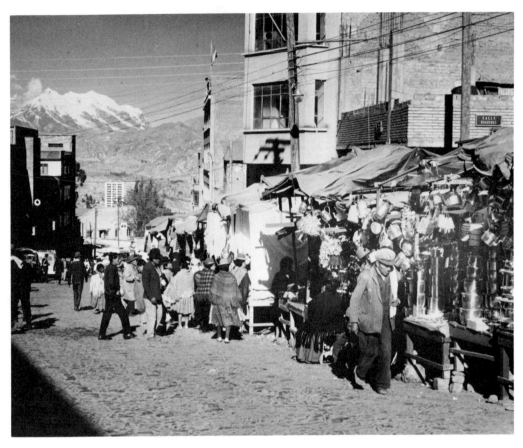

The various races—white, Indian, and mixed—that make up the population of Bolivia may be found in this street market in La Paz.

4. THE PEOPLE

THE TOTAL population of Bolivia is about 5,300,000, of whom more than half are pure Indian. About 35 per cent are *Cholos* (of mixed blood) and 16 per cent are white. The country is underpopulated, and also the population distribution is very uneven, with the high plateau of the Andes, its fertile valleys and sloping hillsides, more densely populated than the rest of the country. Less than one person per square mile (2.5 sq. km.) lives in the hot eastern lowlands.

Bolivia has only a few large cities, and only six have more than 50,000 people. Fully two thirds of the people live in the country, and 42 per cent of the entire population is under 15 years of age (in the United States, only 33 per cent are under 15). The situation in Bolivia is due to two factors—the high birth rate, and the dangers caused by living at a high altitude. The high death rate among infants has also kept the population down. It is very cold in the mountains, especially at night, and many of the poor

A family of Spanish descent, living in Santa Cruz, entertains friends with traditional Spanish hospitality.

peasants do not have enough warm clothing. Most homes in the country have no heat and no sanitary facilities. For these reasons, many babies die before they are a year old. As a result, Bolivia has had a lower rate of growth than Latin America as a whole.

THE WHITE POPULATION

The high altitude discouraged modern Europeans from coming to Bolivia, although a few thousand Germans, Spaniards, and Poles came here in the 1930's, many of them to escape persecution. They settled in the cities of La Paz or Cochabamba, but many of them did not stay and went on to Peru or Argentina.

The whites are mostly descendants of Spaniards who came during the Colonial period.

THE INDIANS

The Indians of Bolivia come from three different ethnic groups: the Quechuas, the Aymaras, and the Guaranis. All three speak different languages, and only 55 per cent speak Spanish at all. Originally the Aymaras formed

At the outdoor Indian market, a young child is left to amuse itself, while its mother tends her stall.

At Tiquipaya, a village in the Cochabamba Valley, volunteer nurses in the Peace Corps admire the baby of a young Quechua Indian woman.

part of a group of people who lived north of Cuzco, Peru. After they became part of the Inca Empire, they settled near Lake Titicaca. Although the Aymaras and the Quechuas have been living in the highlands of Bolivia for centuries, they did not come from a common stock and have never intermixed. The Guaranis live in the lowland regions of the east.

CLOTHING

Despite the inroads of civilization, the Indians cling to their old-time clothes and customs. The women wear their hair in long pigtails, with a soft bowler (derby) hat on top of their head. They wear a bright skirt and a bright

In the heart of La Paz, Indian women wear their traditional fringed shawls and hats. This woman is carrying the proverbial pack on her back, probably with a baby inside. With their shawls, their packs, their many full skirts, and typical hats, the Indian women all dress much alike—there is little chance for originality in fashions that are so rigidly set by custom.

apron and many underskirts, which help to keep them warm and which stand out like hoop skirts. A beautiful fringed Spanish shawl will often wrap around their shoulders and almost always a pack or a baby will be on their back. Indian good-luck dolls, made of clay, come with bundles on their backs. Even in winter, many of the Indian women go barefoot.

While the women keep warm with many petticoats and woollen shawls, the men wear a woollen poncho, often a red one. The Indian men usually wear shoes, and also a *chulo*, or knitted cap that covers their ears. The Indians have unusually large chests, which is Nature's way of allowing them to adapt to living in a high altitude. It is necessary to take in more air in order to get enough oxygen, hence a large chest is an asset. The Indians are usually beardless and broad-faced, and many of them look Oriental.

The men often ride a mule, but the women always walk, usually without swinging their arms. They like to wear a colorful mixture, but always with some garment that is red.

Even in the villages, the Indian women wear the same type of clothing as in the cities, but usually of a less elegant quality. Instead of a shawl, this woman wears a blanket.

DAILY LIFE

Those who have small farms live in adobe houses, with roofs of thatched straw. Those who work in the mines live with their families near the mines, in huts made of stone and mud.

The Indians do their laundry in roadside streams, spreading garments out on the ground to dry in the bright sun. Whatever she is doing and wherever she goes, the Indian woman carries a child on her back, along with supplies and needlework.

For the most part, the white people live in the cities and the Indians and *Cholos* in the country. Although the Agrarian Reform plan gave them small plots of land, the Indians are not very good farmers. The *Cholos* who live in the cities have skilled or semi-skilled jobs, while the whites are in the professions, in business, and in the better paid government jobs.

In the country areas of Bolivia, many of the homes are distinctly primitive, as is this one, made of stones and adobe mixed with straw.

37

New housing has been built in many Bolivian cities, but much remains to be done.

FOOD

In the fertile land around Lake Titicaca, two crops—quinoa and oca—provide the basic food of the Indians. These plants have been raised in Bolivia for hundreds, maybe thousands of years. Quinoa, a relative of spinach, grows 4 or 5 feet (1.2 or 1.5 metres) high, with a heavy head of large seeds. After being toasted and broiled, quinoa makes a delicious porridge—it has a nut-like taste that is different from cereal grains like wheat. Oca, a slender tuber, from 2 to 4 inches (5 to 10 cm.) long, resembling a small pink sausage, is a relative of the familiar wood-sorrel.

The natives of Bolivia have worked out their own way of preserving potatoes and oca for later use. They spread the vegetables on the ground and let them freeze at night and then thaw in the sunlight. Every day for several days the Indians trample them with their bare feet. Finally, only the light dry husk is left and it

A farmer sells his produce— "chuño" and "oca"—in the market in La Paz.

On the Island of the Sun, in Lake Titicaca, these Indians are gathering up the "chuño," or dried, shredded potatoes, which they have been preparing for several days.

will keep for a long time. Travellers carry oca when they are going on a long journey, for it can be cooked quickly.

Potatoes are really the staff of life among the people who live in the Andes. This vegetable will flourish in altitudes above 14,000 feet (4,200 metres). By repeated soaking, freezing, and drying potatoes, the natives make *chuño*, which will keep indefinitely for stews and soups.

A meal for the well-fed might consist of chicken soup, with large pieces of chicken left in it, seasoned with Indian herbs. This is followed by a plate heaped with several slices of roasted hindquarter of kid, plus vegetables covered with a pungent cream sauce. The *chuño* is usually so well disguised that one would never think it is only dried potato. Dessert is baked plantain and freshly picked papayas or other fruit from the tropical valleys.

Cooking in the high plateau region is very different from cooking in the lowlands. At such high altitudes, water boils at a slower rate —on the plateau, it takes 6 minutes to boil a "3-minute" egg.

These women in Potosí have potatoes to sell, as they sit stoically on a pavement in the market where many people pass by.

39

Open-air markets are extremely popular, for they provide opportunities for social gatherings as well as a market place for all needed articles. Here, also, those who seek a cure can find the "travelling doctor."

TRAVELLING DOCTORS

Since there are not enough trained doctors in the highland region, a group of so-called "travelling doctors" make use of folk cures and medicines that are found in the Bolivian highlands. These men travel widely, and some of them even treat white people and *Cholos*. They are said to have a wide control over the supernatural, and many persons insist that they have seen miraculous "cures" performed by one of these "doctors."

Among an illiterate population, these men are a class apart, for they have at least a primary school education, and many have completed secondary school. Perhaps because of their education and lack of common interests with the illiterate Indians, they keep to themselves and do not mix with the natives. In groups of 8 or 10, they travel amazing distances, carrying their "medicines" in picturesque woven bags over their shoulders.

No market or fair would be complete without one of these "doctors" with bundles of leaves, roots, seeds, resins, and charms of bone, wood, or metal spread out before him. Many of his preparations are made up of several plants mixed with fats, powdered bird feathers, hairs, and other ingredients. In addition to his "medicines," the travelling doctor has a number of charms to solve almost any personal difficulty. These are made of stone, roughly carved, and each one is in the form of a hand grasping some object. For example, a hand grasping corn will ensure a good corn crop, and a hand grasping money will guarantee financial success.

Pre-Columbian and Christian traditions merge in many parts of Bolivia. Here a mining official (left) models the traditional Oruro devil's mask, worn by the Oruro Devil Fraternity, of which he is the president. The fraternity is organized to venerate the Virgin of Socavon, patroness of Bolivian miners. Note the replica of a mine entrance, complete with miners. (Right) Folk dancers at Warisata wear traditional masks of a slightly less grotesque style.

A feature of Bolivian festivals is the "piñata," a huge paper container full of toys and trifles, which, when punctured, showers its treasures on the merrymakers.

FIESTAS

The fiestas that come at frequent intervals are mostly of a religious nature, and they provide the background for organized recreation for most of the people. The fiestas are partly supervised by the Catholic Church, to which almost all Bolivians belong, and are held to venerate a particular saint, although the fiesta activities may be as much pagan as Christian. The fiestas are held so frequently that there is scarcely a week in the year when a villager cannot attend one, either in his own or a nearby town.

The fiesta dances are largely of Spanish origin, with local elements added. In the highlands, the *cueca*, or handkerchief dance, is the most popular. In it, the partners circle round and round each other, linking their arms at intervals, much as in an American square dance, while waving a handkerchief in tiny spirals above their heads. The *cueca* is danced at all major fiestas and lasts from mid-morning until early evening.

Many of the churches in Bolivia have remarkably beautiful altars, with decorations in silver and gold. This altar is in the church at Chiautla.

All through the year the miners look forward to the excitement of Carnival, the great fiesta just before Lent. For four days and four nights band music and dancing go on. At the fiesta, the *Cholo* men wear their best suits of black, while the *Cholo* women are gay in vivid full skirts and shawls with bright embroidery.

A family wedding is also the occasion for great merrymaking. After the church service, the couple leads the procession to the home of the bride, where a banquet has been prepared, at the expense of the bridegroom and his parents. Always a generous supply of hard liquor and beer is on hand. A band of musicians provides music for dancing, which continues all day and far into the night.

On the large estates, the seasons for ploughing, planting, and harvesting are also times for festivities. On these occasions, the Indians are given food, drinks, and coca leaves to chew.

In the town of Swapi, a Peace Corps volunteer performs a "Pas de Deux" from the second act of "Swan Lake," with a member of the Bolivian Folk Ballet. The musicians are Peace Corps volunteers serving with the Bolivian National Symphony.

LITERATURE

Colonial literature in Spanish was largely made up of chronicles and religious works written by priests and administrators. The leading Bolivian writer after independence in the 19th century was Gabriel René Moreno, whose works consisted mainly of histories, biographies, literary criticism and vivid descriptions of Bolivian towns and countryside. The early 20th century was dominated by Ricardo Jaime Freyre, a poet greatly influenced by Scandinavian mythology. Among outstanding writers of today are the poet Octavio Campero Echazú, the philosopher Guillermo Francovich, and the essayist and critic Fernando Diez de Medina.

The 18th-century Bolivian artist Melchor Pérez Holguín did this scene of the Holy Family resting during the flight into Egypt.

43

Classes of teenagers often include both boys and girls, and are frequently taught by a priest.

Football (soccer) seems to be a popular sport all over the world, including these Bolivian schoolboys.

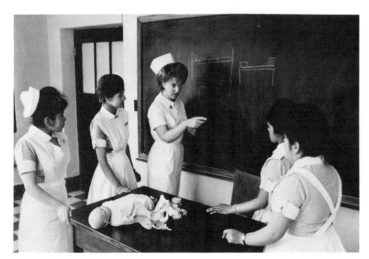

A volunteer nurse from the United States helps train student nurses in La Paz.

These boys are learning to read in a mission school in the rural area.

During the warm weather, classes are held in a covered, but open-air, classroom.

EDUCATION

Primary education is free and compulsory. As a result, the number of adults who can read and write is steadily increasing. Even so, 60 per cent of the people are still illiterate.

Nearly 700,000 pupils attend primary school, and 150,000 attend secondary schools. Besides these, 12,000 students are in vocational schools and 13,500 in the universities. Seven universities exist in Bolivia, one in each of seven departmental capitals.

Not all leisure time is taken up with strenuous athletics. In this rural school, the children have free time for whatever games they like.

A very young pupil is learning her first letters in primary school.

Boxing is a popular activity among the younger generation. Here the teacher is about to call "Time" on the contestants.

Under the Cotoca Project, these Indians (foreground) were moved from arid to fertile land, and have been taught new skills, such as carpentry, to help them build new homes for themselves.

Many of the Indians are extremely eager to learn. This student at Huma Marca is using a makeshift desk in order to carry out his homework assignment.

The biggest educational problem results from the fact that most of the young Indian children cannot speak Spanish. As a result, the teacher must teach them Spanish as a new language when they enter school. Under several relocation projects, adult education is being given to unskilled and illiterate Indians.

Physical education is not neglected in Bolivian schools—these children of Cobija are going through a period of rigorous drill.

At the foot of these high piles of tailings (waste) from the Catavi tin mines, there are many rows of workers' houses.

5. THE ECONOMY

BOLIVIA HAS a wealth of natural resources and could become more than self-sufficient in most essentials. Actually, however, it depends on imports for most of its necessities, due to problems that the country seems unable to solve by itself. The lack of a seaport is one great handicap, while the difficulties of transportation and communication in a mountainous area, plus the extremes of altitude and climate, form another. Foreign trade must pass through the ports of Chile or the river ports on the Amazon.

MINERALS

It is said that a sample of almost every known mineral may be found in the soil of Bolivia. Silver, gold, tin, tungsten, lead, mercury, nickel, antimony, zinc, copper, bismuth, uranium, and iron are among the metals found there. Asbestos, limestone, mica, salt, and sulphur are among the non-metallic minerals in Bolivia. Most of the mining operations occur in a narrow belt, 500 miles (800 km.) long and 60 miles (96 km.) wide, running from north to south along the Cordillera Real. The only metal found in large amounts outside this belt is iron, which is found at Mutun, on the border of Brazil.

The tin-producing countries of Southeast Asia and Africa obtain most of their ore from placer mines, which are near international waterways. Bolivia's tin, on the other hand, is mined from veins and lodes deep underground, at altitudes of from 12,000 to 17,000 feet

Mining for tin at the San José Mine in Oruro requires considerable work above ground as well as underground. The tin concentrate is obtained by "jigging" the ore-bearing material in this device. The tin ore is heavier and settles to the bottom of the jig and the waste is shovelled off the top.

This train at the San José Mine in Oruro carries away the tin ore in very small cars to be processed.

A British engineer (right) visits a family enterprise to observe a sluice box in operation. Tin concentrates are recovered from the water flowing through these sluices.

(3,600 to 5,100 metres) above sea level. Furthermore, they are separated from the point of shipment on the coast by formidable mountain ranges. Another handicap is the fact that the metal content of the ores is decreasing at a rate of 4 per cent each year.

Before 1952, the three largest tin mines were under the control of three families called the "tin barons." They built immense fortunes and controlled much of the country's economic and political life. Foreign engineers were brought in to direct the work and they hired Indians to do the actual mining. After long agitation and discussion, the mines were taken over by the government in 1952, and the "tin barons" lost much of their power.

The famous silver mines of Potosí gave Bolivia its economic start and attracted settlers to this unknown region. Today, tin has replaced silver as the principal mineral asset. Bolivia is the second largest producer of tin in the world, and is the only large-scale source of this metal in the western hemisphere. Two-thirds of its total income from exports come from tin—no other country is so dependent on this one metal.

The government has been trying to promote the mining of other metals, to relieve the almost total dependence upon tin. As a result, the production of bismuth has increased and gold has become an important export. The production of cement has more than doubled since

The Mining and Metallurgical Research Institute at La Paz is carrying out technical and scientific research to improve the mining industry in Bolivia. At the Catavi Mine, one of the largest in Bolivia, workers are clearing a drainage ditch from the side of the mine's railway tracks, as part of an Institute project.

The Cerro Rico Mine near Potosí still produces a small amount of silver.

the 1950's. Today the chief exports are tin, antimony, tungsten, and silver, which are sold largely to Great Britain, the United States, and Argentina.

In the refinery in Santa Cruz, an operator makes notes of the gauge readings.

OIL AND GAS

The first indications that petroleum was under Bolivian soil appeared in 1895, but no oil concessions were granted until 1916. Not until 1925 was the actual existence of "black gold" confirmed. This was in the concessions held by the Standard Oil Company. The principal oil fields were in the districts of Santa Cruz, Chuquisaca, and Tarija. Production, refining, and export of oil was put in the hands of a Bolivian firm in December, 1936. The following year, the concessions given to the Standard Oil Company in 1921 were withdrawn and became the property of the government. In 1969, the concessions previously given to the Bolivian Gulf Oil Company were nationalized, and the entire operation is now in the hands of the government.

Total production of oil exceeds 40,000 barrels daily, and part of this is exported to Argentina. A refinery in Cochabamba has a capacity of 8,000 barrels daily, and crude oil is pumped to it from Camiri. Bolivia thus produces sufficient gasoline, kerosene, and lubricants for its own use, and it is hoped that soon there will be enough for export. There are small refineries in Sucre, Santa Cruz, Camiri, and Ber-

A vertical view shows the inside of a drilling rig at a site in Naranjilios, where a team of drillers are changing a drilling bit.

mejo. In Cochabamba a factory now produces containers for gasoline and lubricants.

Plans have been made for building petro-chemical plants, so that national gas may be sold and sent to Argentina. A gas pipeline is being built from Santa Cruz to Yacuiba, financed by a grant from the Bank for International Development.

AGRICULTURE

The farm land, like the mines, was formerly held almost entirely by a few rich families. The injustices, poverty, and hunger resulting from this system helped to bring on revolution in 1952. The following year, the Land Reform Act went into effect, similar to earlier land reforms in Mexico and Guatemala. As a result, the peasants were given land of their own, but the old-fashioned methods of farming did not change. Even though they now own small tracts of land, the peasants are bound by tradition and handicapped by illiteracy. Land is in great demand, but often the farming units are so small as to be uneconomical to operate. The government is seeking to help the farmers, through vocational education, technical assistance, and improvements in transportation.

Coca, the most important crop of Bolivia—about 1,000,000 pounds (400,000 kg.) of coca leaves are exported every year—is used to

In this simple mill near Trinidad, the sugar cane is ground. A young driver guides the two horses that supply the motor power for the mill.

Improved maize (corn) culture is one of the objectives of the Paracaya Project near Cochabamba.

Women harvest coca leaves near Caroica. The leaves are chewed by the Indians as a stimulant.

An Indian woman wields her hoe with one hand, while clutching her child with the other.

Earth-moving equipment is inspected at a resettlement site in the lowlands. The Bolivian government has been engaged for some years in developing large scale plans for resettling people from the poor lands of the Altiplano in the rich but undeveloped lands of the Amazon region.

make the drug cocaine, which is used to deaden pain. The Indians like to chew the leaves, and it is thought that they acquired the habit in order to deaden the pangs of hunger. Small quantities of coca leaves, however, serve to keep the body warm and act as a stimulant—quite the opposite effect from deadening.

The government has carried out numerous experiments to improve agriculture and living standards in the Altiplano. These studies have been made jointly with the governments of Peru and Ecuador and are known collectively as the Andean Indian Project. Here an agronomist instructs Indian farmers in the use of tractors.

The bicycle is a symbol of progress in the Altiplano. These young "campesinos" (rural dwellers) have cycled from their farm homes to attend a meeting of community leaders conducted by a United Nations expert (second from right).

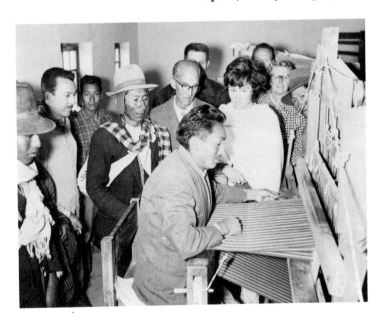

The Andean Indian Project also conducts handicraft workshops where Indians acquire such skills as weaving.

A llama train threads its way over the mountain. These tame, useful beasts of burden are a mainstay of the economy of the Indians.

A livestock specialist shows shepherds how to use the dredging gun, a device which rids sheep of intestinal parasites.

Two oxen pull the crude plough that makes a single furrow, while the woman walks behind, planting the seed.

A modern milk-processing plant is located at Cochabamba, in the heart of one of the best dairy regions of South America.

The area around Santa Cruz now produces enough rice and sugar cane for its own needs, with a small surplus for export. Sugar cane was introduced to Bolivia at an early date, but much of it has always been used for making rum.

The agriculture of the valleys, which cover about 14 per cent of the total area of the country, has wide variations, depending on the altitude and latitude. The valleys northeast of La Paz, called the *Yungas*, have better soils than the valleys of the highlands, and also have easy access to the city. Besides the staple foods which the peasants eat, such commercial crops as cacao, coca, and coffee are produced in this area, as well as tropical fruits and cassava.

In the basins and valleys near Cochabamba, fairly good soils enable the farmers to grow wheat, corn, and barley, as well as vegetables and tropical fruits, which are sold to the cities in the highlands.

Valleys to the south are less densely populated and grow few crops for the market. Near such large cities as Sucre and Tarija, however, cereals and fruits are grown. Cattle and goats are raised and furnish meat and milk for the market.

The tropical lowlands in the east are the least developed, and it is not known what farming possibilities they may have. Of the 190,000,000 acres (760,000,000 hectares) in these lowlands, only about 140,000 acres (560,000 hectares) are under cultivation, mostly near Santa Cruz.

LIVESTOCK

The domesticated llama and alpaca have been used by the highland Indians since prehistoric times. These animals are similar to the camel in their endurance and usefulness in transportation. Their wool is used for making clothing, especially fine coats, and for cordage, their meat dried and conserved, but seldom eaten fresh.

Cattle are raised in many parts of Bolivia. In the highlands and the high valleys, oxen are used for drawing wagons. When no longer useful, these animals are killed and used for food. In a few areas of the lowlands, mostly near El Beni and Santa Cruz, cattle breeding for beef is carried out on a large scale.

Sheep are raised mostly in the highlands, where they can graze freely on natural pastures the year round. The chinchilla, a native rodent prized for its luxurious fur, is also raised and its skins exported. Other livestock, grown on a smaller scale, include horses, mules, donkeys, pigs, goats, rabbits, guinea pigs (for food), chickens, turkeys, and ducks.

FORESTRY

Although Bolivia has great timber resources, among the best in the world, there is little consumption of wood and almost no exports of it.

In the highlands there are occasional euca-

The Amazonian forests are rich in hardwood trees, but the timber industry remains to be fully developed. It is growing, however, as more and more Indians from the Altiplano are settled in the lowlands.

lyptus groves near the cities—the eucalyptus was introduced from its native Australia in the 19th century. Some eucalyptus trees are grown for fuel and for supports in mines, near Cochabamba and Sucre. The best forests, however, are found on the eastern slopes of the Andes and along the rivers of the Amazon basin. Here are large areas of tropical trees, both evergreens and hardwoods.

Rubber of high quality, which grows wild in the forests of Pando and Beni, is the chief forest export. Brazil nuts, which grow wild on trees often 100 feet (30 metres) tall, are the second most important forest export. In parts of southeast Bolivia are forests of abundant hardwoods, such as walnut and mahogany. Most of the country's huge timber resources are beyond the reach of modern means of transportation, however.

The number of factories is gradually increasing, and more and more products are being made in Bolivia. The picture shows a man handling some complicated machinery in a foundry.

FISHING

The rivers and lakes of Bolivia are well stocked with a large variety of fish which are caught and eaten by the people living in the area. There is commercial fishing in Lake Titicaca, however—rainbow trout and *boga*, a small bass-like fish, are supplied to the market of La Paz. During the season, fish are taken from the Pilcomayo River in the south and shipped to Potosí, Sucre, Tarija, and Cochabamba.

MANUFACTURES

In the 1960's, the production of raw cotton rose considerably and this led to an increase in manufactured cotton products. Also in the 1960's, the government took a more friendly attitude toward private enterprise, which led to the development of many small factories. Cement factories, food-processing plants, shoe factories, and various other new industries were introduced, and hydro-electric plants were built in La Paz and Cochabamba.

In 1967, Bolivia joined the Latin American

At this plant in the small Bolivian community of Comarapa, tires are repaired and given new treads.

Free Trade Association and also the regional Andean Group, hoping to improve its economic position through these organizations.

TRANSPORTATION

Bolivia, like other Andean countries, has changed during the 20th century from ox-cart to aircraft. The nation is served efficiently by several international airlines that land at El Alto Airport, the highest commercial airport in the world. Only 5 miles (8 km.) from the city of La Paz, El Alto is 12,000 feet (3,600 metres) above sea level!

The Bolivian National Airline connects cities throughout the highlands and plains and also has flights to nearby countries. Air transportation is of vital importance to Bolivia because of its inland location and the scarcity of trains and good roads.

The Pan American Highway, linking Argentina and Peru, crosses Bolivia from the northwest to the south, passing through the districts of Tarica, Chuquisaca, Potosí, Oruro, and La Paz. It is possible to use this road at all times of the year except the rainy season.

The major cities of the Altiplano are now linked by rail. This train has stopped at a point near Cochabamba, and some of the passengers have come out to take a stretch.

Timber is being unloaded from the small freight cars in the yard of this mill in Trinidad.

MANPOWER

About 1,000,000 Bolivians were gainfully employed in the 1960's. Of this total, 63 per cent were engaged in farming, hunting, and fishing, while the others worked in mines and quarries, in manufacturing and construction, in sanitary services and miscellaneous occupations.

Bolivia has not developed as much as many other South American countries—the people still cling to the old-time ways of doing things, especially on the farms. With old-fashioned wooden ploughs they scratch a furrow 4 inches (10 cm.) deep. The bulls pull the ploughs hitched only with ropes tied around their horns —there is no yoke. Women follow the plough, breaking up the heavy clods of earth by beating them with stones tied on sticks.

TRADE UNIONS

Up until 1943, trade unions were illegal in Bolivia, but since that date they have become very strong and active. Besides trying to improve the working conditions, including the length of a working day as well as the wage rates, the unions have been trying to stop the practice of paying workers, in part, by giving them coca, a habit-forming drug. All these aspects of the economic life of the country have become bitter political issues. Through the years, the tin miners have taken the lead in seeking to gain various reforms.

AID FROM THE UNITED STATES

Great prosperity came with World War II and its demand for two important Bolivian products—tin and wolframite (from which the metal tungsten is extracted). Rising prices and strikes led to the growth of the leftist National Revolutionary Movement. When the Bolivian economy collapsed in 1953, a dreadful inflation followed. This was caused by the government's

When goods and people must travel over winding roads through terrain like this, it is not surprising that Bolivia has been slow to develop.

This Indian, living on the Island of the Sun in Lake Titicaca, is working an elaborate loom. Although he wears a knitted cap that covers his ears, his feet are bare.

Ploughing is still done largely by oxen at Chambi, a farming community in the Pillapi Experimental Project.

costly social-welfare scheme, and by continual wage increases. Fearing that Bolivia would turn to Communism, in 1953, the United States started giving financial aid. In 1956, a stabilization plan was begun, in collaboration with the United States and the International Monetary Fund. Wages were frozen for one year. In 1963, a new currency was introduced.

During the 1960's, the United States channelled its aid toward specific development projects. However, in 1967, the United States withdrew its grants in support of the Bolivian budget. This withdrawal of funds, plus the heavy expense of the anti-guerrilla campaign, resulted in a large budget deficit. The foreign debt was approaching U.S. $400,000,000 at the time.

To check the growth of debt, in 1968 public expenditure was severely cut, various taxes were imposed, and strict controls were placed on government agencies. A special United

A Peace Corps worker (left) works in the Alto Beni region, where he helps in the resettlement of Andean Indians in new homes in the Amazon lowlands.

Two-wheeled carts drawn by oxen are still a common sight in parts of Bolivia, as here in Trinidad, a city in the Amazonian lowlands.

Oil is pumped through a series of pipes from the wells to these huge storage tanks near Cochabamba.

States AID (Agency for International Development) grant of U.S. $12,000,000 was obtained to help support the budget. The government restricted wage increases in all sectors of the economy, an import ban was imposed on motor cars for one year, and attempts were made to check the large contraband trade.

TOURISM

Bolivia offers many delights to the visitor. Sportsmen will be attracted to Lake Titicaca, where there is excellent trout fishing and an abundance of ducks and partridge in the surrounding countryside.

About 40 miles (64 km.) from the city of La Paz, the ruins of Tiahuanaco, on the border of Lake Titicaca, can easily be reached by railway or by road at any time of the year.

Copacabana, also on the shores of Lake Titicaca, existed at the time of the Incas and served as a place of recreation for the Inca royal family. Copacabana is famous for the sanctuary built in the early 17th century in homage to the Virgin of Copacabana. Carved in wood by a local artist, Tito Yupanqui, the statue of the Virgin is believed to have miraculous powers and is venerated by the people of Bolivia and southern Peru. The shrine constructed there is a beautiful example of colonial architecture, built by the Dominican missionaries in 1652. In the temple are many valuable paintings and also priceless jewels, which have been offered to the Virgin by the people.

The climate of the Lake Titicaca area is pleasant throughout the year, and in October, November, and December the water is warm enough for swimming. At different times of the year there are pilgrimages to the Sanctuary, especially during religious festivals, when the folk dances and the picturesque costumes of the people make an attractive spectacle.

The places of major tourist interest are all fairly near the city of La Paz, which is the hub of activities in Bolivia. There are interesting places for the traveller in other parts of the republic, but they are not so easily reached.

About 20 miles (32 km.) from La Paz are the ski slopes of Chacaltaya. Here skiing is good throughout the entire winter season. In Chacaltaya, the Andino Boliviano Club offers accommodation to tourists and visitors. This is an ideal location for admiring the beauty of the Andes and their highest peaks.

A few hours drive on a well built road brings one to the *Yungas*, the land of small sloping plains, just a few hundred feet above sea level. In this lower altitude, the climate is much warmer. In such towns as Coroica (60 miles or 96 km. from La Paz) and Chulumani (85 miles or 136 km.) there are good hotels with swimming pools where one may swim throughout the year.

Only 60 miles (96 km.) from La Paz, on the road to Oruro, are the thermal baths of Urmiri, while a few miles farther on are the baths of Viscachani. Located in both places are good hotels with swimming pools and medicinal

Tourists from all parts of the world can easily reach Bolivia by international airlines. The airport at La Paz is the highest in the world.

heated waters. Many people go to these places for the treatment of rheumatism and other ailments.

The plateaus between the majestic mountain ranges of the Andes offer the visitor panoramic views of unusual beauty, with the summits constantly snow-covered and the climate fresh in the summer. The deep and welcoming green valleys of Cochabamba, Sucre, Tarija, Sorata, and many others offer the visitor the traditional hospitality of their people, inherited from Spanish ancestors. The vast plains of the east and northwest, with their exuberant tropical vegetation, have an abundance of game and fish. They are a source of delight both to the tourist and the explorer. Each area of Bolivia has some special offering for the visitor.

INDEX

CITIES, 13–22, 34
CLIMATE, 9, 12, 13, 18, 19
CLOTHING, 6, 9, 15, 18, 36, 37, 42, 61
Cobija, 21
Coca, 42, 52–54, 57, 60
Cocaine, 52–54
Cochabamba, 18–19, 26, 35, 52, 53, 57
Coffee, 57
Colombia, 26
THE COLONIAL ERA, 24–25, 35
Columbus, Christopher, 24
Communism, 28, 29, 33, 61
Condor, 12
Congress Building, 18, 30
Copacabana, 26, 62–63
Copper, 20
Cordillera, see Mountains
Corregidor, 31
Cotoca Project, 46
Creoles, 26
Cuba, 28, 29, 33
Cueca, 41
DAILY LIFE, 37
Dance, 41, 43
De Almagio, Diego, 24
De Mendoza, Alonso, 13
De Sucre, General Antonio José, 18, 25, 26, 27
Devil's mask, 41
Diez de Medina, Fernando, 43
Doctors, travelling, 40
THE ECONOMY, 48–63
Ecuador, 26
EDUCATION, 44–47
Eucalyptus, 58
Exports, 50, 51
FIESTAS, 41–42
FISHING, 59
FLORA AND FAUNA, 10–12
FOOD, 38–39
FORESTRY, 12, 57
Francovich, Guillermo, 43
Freyre, Ricardo Jaime, 43
Gas, 51
Gate of the Sun, 22, 23
GOVERNMENT, 30–33
Government by decree, 30
"Granary of Bolivia," 18
Guanaco, 10, 12
Guaranis, 35–36
Guerrilla Warfare, 29
Guevara, Che, 28, 29
Haciendas, 25
Handicrafts, 55, 61
Handkerchief dance, 41
Highlands, see Altiplano
HISTORY, 23–29
Housing, 7, 9, 16, 17, 20, 25, 35, 37, 38, 46, 48, 61
Huallpa, Diego, 20
Hydro-electric plants, 59
Illiteracy, 31, 40, 45, 47, 53
THE INCA EMPIRE, 24, 25, 36
Incas, 22, 26, 62–63
Independence, 18, 26
THE INDIANS, 6, 7, 9, 13, 14–15, 16, 17, 23–25, 27, 28, 31, 35–42
Aymaras, 35–36
Guaranis, 35–36
Quechuas, 35–36
Institute of Metallurgical Investigation, 20
Inter-American Development Bank, 33
International Monetary Fund, 61
Island of the Sun and the Moon, 10, 61

Jesuits, 21
Junin, 26
Kollasuyu, 24
LAKE POOPÓ, 10, 19
LAKE TITICACA, 9–10, 11, 23, 36, 61, 62–63
THE LAND, 5–22
Land Reform Act, 52
La Paz, 5, 13, 25, 26, 27, 30, 31, 32, 34, 63
LA PAZ, IMPORTANCE OF, 32
Latin America Free Trade Association, 59
League of Nations, 27
LITERATURE, 43
LIVESTOCK, 57, see also Cattle
Llamas, 3, 10, 11, 56, 57
LLANOS, 8, 12, 34, 36, 57
THE LOWLANDS, see Llanos
MANPOWER, 60
MANUFACTURES, 58, 59
Map, 4
Markets, 13, 14, 15, 34, 35, 38, 39, 40
Masks, 41
MINERALS, 48–51
Mining, 6, 19–20, 21, 24, 28, 33, 41, 48–51
The Mining and Metallurgical Research Institute, 50
Miraflores, 16
Missionaries, 21, 63
Moreno, Gabriel René, 43
Mountain Ranges, 5–8, 7, 9, 13, 24, 25, 63
Cordillera Occidental, 5, 7
Cordillera Oriental, 7
Cordillera Real, 7, 48
Mountains
Ancohuma, 7
Illimani, 5, 7
Sajama, 7
Tocorpuri, 7
National Congress, 16
National Revolutionary Movement, 28, 60
Nitrate, 28
Oca, 38–39
Ocllo, Mama, 24
OIL AND GAS, 21, 27, 28, 51–52, 62
Oruro, 19–20, 26, 41, 49
Oruro Devil Fraternity, 41
Ovando Candia, General Alfredo, 28–29
Painting, 43
Pan American Highway, 59
Paracaya Project, 53
Paraguay, 5, 8, 27, 33
war with, 27
Paz, Victor, 30
Peace Corps, 33, 36, 43, 61
Penaranda, General Enrique, 27
THE PEOPLE, 34–47
Pereda Asbún, General Juan, 29
Perón, Juan, 29
Peru, 5, 9, 26, 35
Pillapi Experimental Project, 61
"Piñata," 41
Pizarro, Francisco, 24
Plateaus, 7, see also Altiplano
POLITICAL PARTIES, 32–33
Population, 34
Potatoes, 39
Potosí, 20–21, 24–25, 26, 50
Prefect, 31
Presidential Palace, 15–16
Quechuas, 35–36

Quinine, 12
Quinoa, 38
Railways, 26, 28, 33, 59
Resettlement, 28, 46, 47, 52, 54, 58, 61
THE REPUBLIC, 26–27
THE REVOLUTION OF 1952, 28–29
Rivers
Amazon, 8
Madeira, 8
Plata, 8
Rubber, 12, 21, 26, 58
Ruins, 21, 22, 23, 24, 62
Salas de Uyuni, 10
Salinas, Luis Adolfo Siles, 28
San José Mine, 49
Santa Cruz, 7, 18, 19, 26, 51, 57
Santa Cruz, Andres, 26
Seacoast, loss of, 26, 28
Seasons, 9
Secessionists, 27
Senate, 30, 31
Sheep, 6, 11, 12, 56, 57
Silver, 19, 21, 25, 50
Social Security, 32
Spanish influences, 35, 63
Spanish language, 28, 35, 47
Spanish rule, 24–26
Sports, 44, 46, 62–63
Standard Oil Company, 51
Sucre, 18, 25, 31, 51, 57
SUFFRAGE, 31
Sugar, 21, 57
Supreme Court, 18, 31
Surazos, 19
Swamps, 8
Tarija, 21, 51, 57
Technical University of St. Augustine, 20
Thermal baths, 20, 63
Tiahuanaco, 21–22, 23, 62
Tiahuanacotas, 23
Tin, 20, 21, 27, 33, 48, 49, 50, 60
"Tin barons," 50
Torres, General Juan José, 29, 33
Totora, 10
TOURISM, 62–63
Trade Unions, 60
TRANSPORTATION, 11, 48, 52, 56, 58, 59, 60, 62, 63
TRAVELLING DOCTORS, 40
Trees
Cinchona, 12
Eucalyptus, 58
Rubber, 12, 21, 26, 58
Trinidad, 21, 62
Universities, 16–17, 18, 20, 45
Upper Peru, 25, 26
Urmiri, 63
Venezuela, 26
Vicuña, 10, 12
Vinto, 33
Virgin of Copacabana, 63
Virgin of Socavon, 41
Viscachani, 63
THE WAR OF INDEPENDENCE, 26
WELFARE SERVICES, 32
THE WHITE POPULATION, 35
Wolframite, 60
Women, 6, 15, 31, 36, 37, 39, 53, 56, 60
Wool, 6, 11, 12
World War I, 27
Writers, 43
Yacuiba, 52
THE YUNGAS, 7–8, 57, 63
Yungay, battle of, 26

Acre, 26–27
Adobe houses, 9, 37
Agrarian Reform, 37
AGRICULTURE, 7–8, 52–54
AID FROM THE UNITED STATES, 60–63
Alpaca, 10, 11, 57
ALTIPLANO, 6, 7, 8, 11, 34, 36, 54, 55
Altitude, living conditions at, 7, 13, 17, 34–35, 36
Andean Group, 59
Andean Indian Project, 54, 55
Andes, see Mountain Ranges
Andino Boliviano Club, 63
Antofagasta, 28
Architecture, 16, 17, 18, 19, 20, 23, 24, 25, 26, 31, 42, 63
Area, 5
Argentina, 5, 8, 29, 33, 35, 51
Arica, 26
Army, 32
Atacama, 28
Atahuallpa, 24
Ayacucho, battle of, 26
Aymaras, 35–36
Balsa canoes, 10, 11
Bank for International Development, 52
Bánzer Suárez, General Hugo, 29, 30, 33
Barrientos, General René, 28
Birth rate, 34
Boga, 59
Bolívar, General Simón, 26, 27
Bolivian Gulf Oil Company, 33, 51
Bolivian National Airline, 59
Bolivian National Symphony, 43
Boundaries, 5, 27, 28
loss of territories, 26, 28
Brazil, 5, 8, 12, 21, 26–27, 33
Calahumana, Maria, 26
Camiri, 51
Campero Echazú, Octavio, 43
Campesinos, 55
Cantons, 31
Capital, 13, 16, 31
Capac, Manco, 24
Carnival, 41–42
Castro, Fidel, 28, 29
Catavi tin mines, 48, 50
Catholic Church, 41
Cattle, 7, 21, 27, 57
Cerro Rico Mine, 51
Chaco, Gran, 8, 27, 28
THE CHACO WAR, 27, 28
Chamber of Deputies, 30, 31
Charcas, 25
Children, 8, 9, 34, 35, 36, 37, 39, 44–47, 53
Chile, 5, 26
Chinchilla, 57
Cholos, 13, 27, 32, 34, 37, 39, 42
Chulo, 36
Chuño, 38, 39
Chuquisaca, 26, 51
Churches, 15, 16, 17, 19, 20, 26, 42, 63